ANIMAL SAFARI

Giant Pandas

by Kari Schuetz

BELLWETHER MEDIA · MINNEAPOLIS, MN

Note to Librarians, Teachers, and Parents:

Blastoff! Readers are carefully developed by literacy experts and combine standards-based content with developmentally appropriate text.

Level 1 provides the most support through repetition of high-frequency words, light text, predictable sentence patterns, and strong visual support.

Level 2 offers early readers a bit more challenge through varied simple sentences, increased text load, and less repetition of high-frequency words.

Level 3 advances early-fluent readers toward fluency through increased text and concept load, less reliance on visuals, longer sentences, and more literary language.

Level 4 builds reading stamina by providing more text per page, increased use of punctuation, greater variation in sentence patterns, and increasingly challenging vocabulary.

Level 5 encourages children to move from "learning to read" to "reading to learn" by providing even more text, varied writing styles, and less familiar topics.

Whichever book is right for your reader, Blastoff! Readers are the perfect books to build confidence and encourage a love of reading that will last a lifetime!

This edition first published in 2012 by Bellwether Media, Inc.

No part of this publication may be reproduced in whole or in part without written permission of the publisher. For information regarding permission, write to Bellwether Media, Inc., Attention: Permissions Department, 5357 Penn Avenue South, Minneapolis, MN 55419.

Library of Congress Cataloging-in-Publication Data
Schuetz, Kari.
Giant pandas / by Kari Schuetz.
  p. cm. – (Blastoff! readers. animal safari)
Includes bibliographical references and index.
Summary: "Developed by literacy experts for students in kindergarten through grade three, this book introduces giant pandas to young readers through leveled text and related photos"–Provided by publisher.
ISBN 978-1-60014-603-9 (hardcover : alk. paper)
 1. Giant panda–Juvenile literature. I. Title.
QL737.C27S35 2012
599.789–dc22
                                    2011007391

Printed in the United States of America, North Mankato, MN.

080111   1187

Contents

What Are Giant Pandas?   4

Where Giant Pandas Live   8

Bamboo   12

Baby Pandas   18

Glossary   22

To Learn More   23

Index   24

What Are Giant Pandas?

Giant pandas are bears with black and white fur.

They are very **rare**. Fewer than 2,000 giant pandas remain in the **wild**.

Where Giant Pandas Live

Giant pandas
live in forests
on mountains.

They spend a lot
of time alone.

Bamboo

Giant pandas
spend half
of every day
eating **bamboo**.

bamboo

13

Giant pandas sit down to eat. They hold bamboo between their paws and **wrists**.

Giant pandas chew bamboo with their strong **jaws** and flat teeth.

Baby Pandas

Baby giant pandas stay with their mothers for up to three years.

They begin to
climb trees when
they are about
five months old.
Be careful panda!

Glossary

bamboo—plants with hollow stems

jaws—the bones that form the mouths of some animals

rare—few in number

wild—natural land that has not been disturbed

wrists—bones that connect the hands and arms

To Learn More

AT THE LIBRARY

Dowson, Nick. *Tracks of a Panda.* Cambridge, Mass.: Candlewick Press, 2007.

Keller, Susanna. *Meet the Panda.* New York, N.Y.: PowerKids Press, 2010.

Schreiber, Anne. *Pandas.* Washington, D.C.: National Geographic, 2010.

ON THE WEB

Learning more about giant pandas is as easy as 1, 2, 3.

1. Go to www.factsurfer.com.

2. Enter "giant pandas" into the search box.

3. Click the "Surf" button and you will see a list of related Web sites.

With factsurfer.com, finding more information is just a click away.

Index

alone, 10

baby, 18

bamboo, 12, 13, 14, 16

black, 4

careful, 20

chew, 16

climb, 20

day, 12

eating, 12, 14

flat, 16

forests, 8

fur, 4

hold, 14

jaws, 16

months, 20

mothers, 18

mountains, 8

paws, 14

rare, 6

sit, 14

teeth, 16

time, 10

trees, 20

white, 4

wild, 6

wrists, 14

years, 18

The images in this book are reproduced through the courtesy of: Olga Khoroshunova, front cover; Michael Krabs/Age Fotostock, pp. 5, 21; Eric Baccega/Age Fotostock, p. 7; Jean-Paul Ferrero/Auscape/Minden Pictures, p. 9; Shigeki Tanaka/Age Fotostock, p. 11; Tom & Pat Leeson/KimballStock, p. 13; Subbotina Anna, p. 13 (small); Lynn M. Stone/naturepl.com, p. 15; Bryan Faust, p. 17; Kenneth W. Fink/ardea.com, p. 19.